Crown Imperial

(Coronation March, 1937)

WILLIAM WALTON
arr. Herbert Murrill

This arrangement incorporates the cuts made by the composer in 1963. A shorter version can be played by starting from the main theme at bar 176, cutting back from bar 209 to bar 89, and continuing from there through to the end.

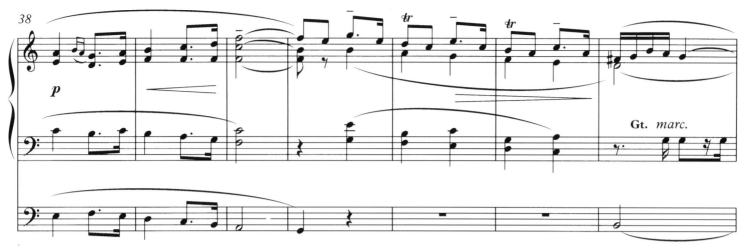

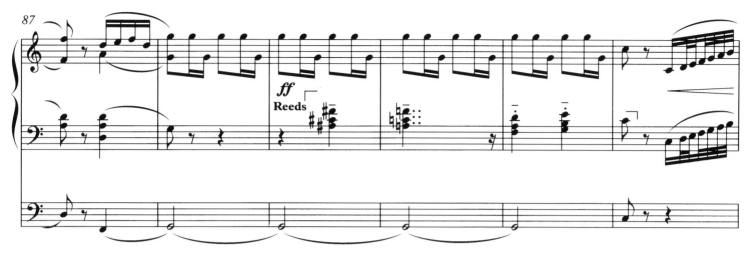

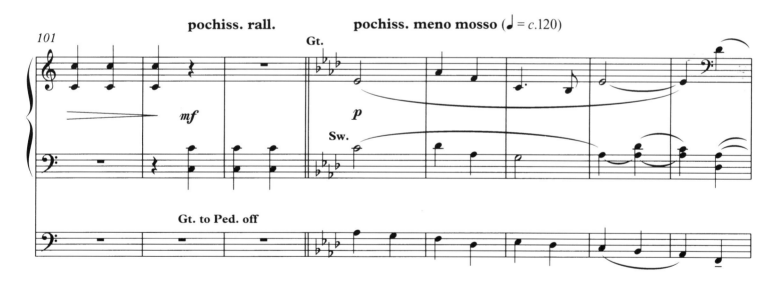

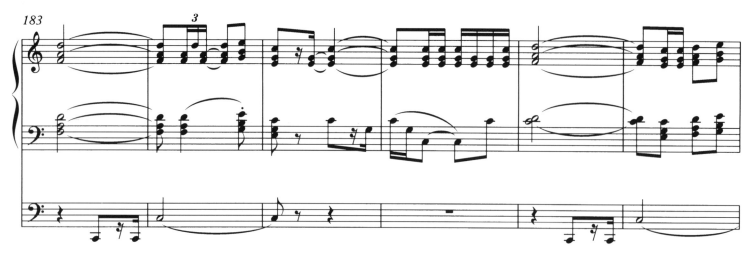

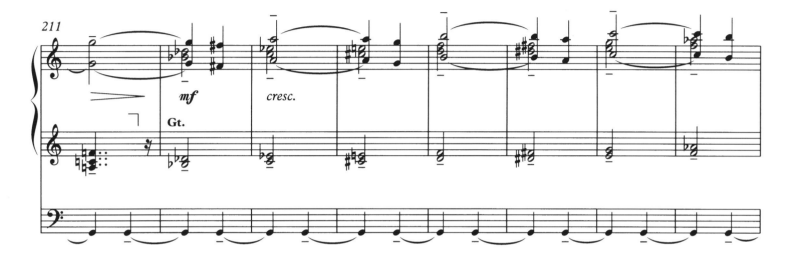

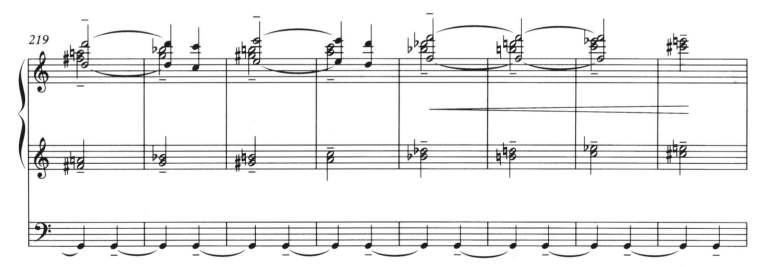

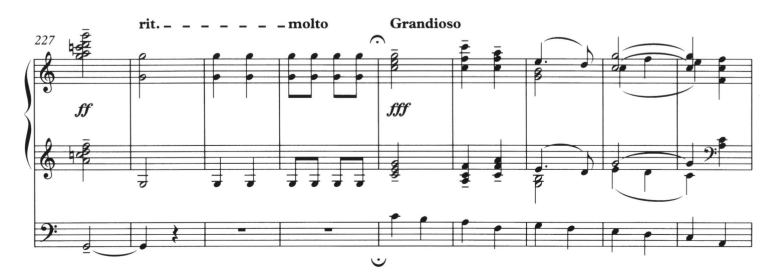

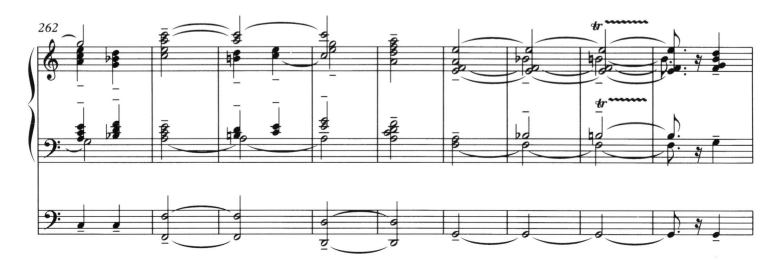

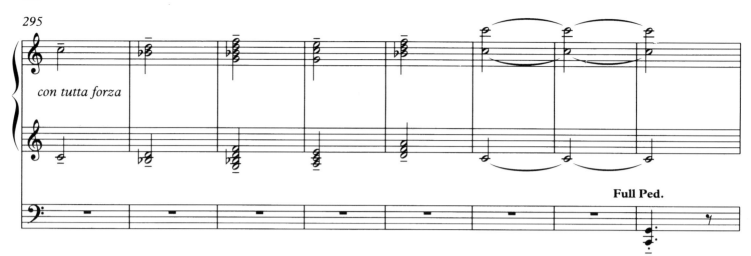

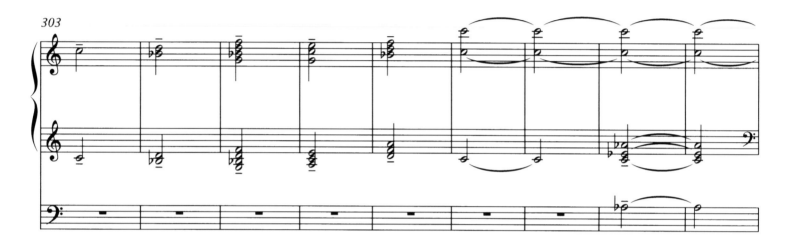

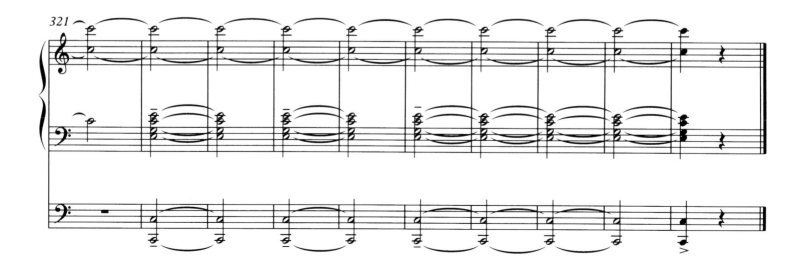